TWO LECTURES
ON THE
SCIENCE OF LANGUAGE

T0370861

TWO LECTURES

ON THE

SCIENCE OF LANGUAGE

by

JAMES HOPE MOULTON, M.A., D.Lit. (Lond.)

Late Fellow of King's College, Cambridge,
Tutor at the Didsbury Theological College, Manchester,
Late Senior Classical Master at The Leys School, Cambridge.

Cambridge
at the University Press
1903

CAMBRIDGE
UNIVERSITY PRESS

University Printing House, Cambridge CB2 8BS, United Kingdom

Published in the United States of America by Cambridge University Press, New York

Cambridge University Press is part of the University of Cambridge.

It furthers the University's mission by disseminating knowledge in the pursuit of
education, learning and research at the highest international levels of excellence.

www.cambridge.org
Information on this title: www.cambridge.org/9781107660953

First published 1903
First paperback edition 2014

A catalogue record for this publication is available from the British Library

ISBN 978-1-107-66095-3 Paperback

IOANNI PEILE, Litt. D.

ΤΡΟΦΕΙΑ

PREFACE.

THIS little book consists of two lectures delivered on August 19th and 20th, 1902, to students of the University Extension at Cambridge. In deference to the kindly expressed wish of many in my audience, and in view of the non-existence (so far as I know) of anything in English giving a purely popular introduction to the Science of Language in its latest developments, I ventured to offer the lectures to the University Press for publication, hoping that they might serve to stimulate interest in a most fascinating study, sadly neglected in this country. I was encouraged in this resolution by my friend Professor Ridgeway, who very kindly read the lectures in MS. and helped me with many suggestions. The first lecture is printed nearly as delivered; the second, which was given extempore, was written out immediately after, and follows the general lines of my notes. I have added a brief Bibliography for those who may be tempted to pursue the study. It seemed best to preserve the lecture form, which to some extent mitigates the apparent absurdity of putting such a title as "The Science of Language" over a booklet of fifty or sixty pages. There are many things here which would be out of place in a scientific summary : there are many things absent which even an article for a small encyclopaedia ought to contain. Popular lectures will only be expected to include what will rouse interest and lead to further reading. As such I venture to put forth what is almost the only published product of my sixteen years' teaching in Cambridge, so far as the general subject is concerned. Writing from a new sphere, where Hellenistic Greek will claim yet more rigorously the time that might have been given to Comparative Philology, I feel as if I were hanging a *votiva tabula* in the temple of Aius Locutius—if that shadowy divinity may be persuaded to take under his patronage a subject so clearly appropriate to him.

It only remains to express my gratitude to some of my old Cambridge friends for obligations very deeply felt. The Master of Christ's, who has kindly allowed me to inscribe these lectures to him, was the teacher to whom, in undergraduate days, I owed my introduction to the "New Grammarians," then very new. Aius Locutius has long received Dr Peile's votive tablet, to the sincere regret of all his old pupils, who will not forget the lucidity, wide knowledge, and unfailing judgment which always informed his lectures. His successor in the Readership of Comparative Philology, Mr Giles, has most kindly read my proofs and helped me with a number of suggestions. His learning and acuteness have been an invaluable help to me, as most of my pages would show if space permitted separate mention of the modifications due to his criticism. I need not say, however, that the responsibility for statements made here remains wholly my own. I have also been helped, not for the first time, by my old friend and colleague, Mr E. E. Kellett, of The Leys, who has carefully read the proofs. The last acknowledgement, alas! is one which its recipient is no longer here to see. Professor Cowell, with whom I had the privilege of reading for a short time in Sanskrit, and for some fifteen years in Zend, leaves a venerated memory behind for all who received out of his boundless stores. What he knew not was not knowledge, in Aryan subjects certainly, and in many other fields; but his pupils always had to struggle with the impression that they were there really to impart information to him. The man in the street knows of him as the "onlie begetter" of

Fitzgerald's Omar. Happily there are scholars enough left to preserve in grateful memory more solid titles to the fame of the greatest English Orientalist of his time.

I should like to have named in closing at least two other great scholars whose friendship, though their work lies in very different fields, has been a powerful stimulus to me. But since their influence on this little book is only indirect, it seems hardly fair to make them apparent contributories. I must be content with merging these debts in the comprehensive acknowledgement to the *genius loci*, whose influence is realised most keenly when a long residence in Cambridge is just closed. I would that my parting tribute were worthier of the shrine.

J. H. M.

DIDSBURY,
March, 1903.

I. THE SCIENCE OF LANGUAGE.

THERE are very few sciences for which the Nineteenth Century did as much as it did for the Science of Language. It is indeed a question whether there was such a thing as a *science* of language till the eve of the "Wonderful Century," unless the stage of rudimentary guesswork in which this like other sciences began is to be called "science" by anticipation. In the eighteenth century etymology was defined as a science in which the vowels mattered nothing at all, and the consonants very little. Now, we are no longer allowed to indulge in wild guesses when we seek the history of a familiar word. We have to bind ourselves rigidly within the laws of an exact scientific method, and the science is the more complicated and exacting in that it cannot confine itself to mechanical processes which may be measured and analysed like those of chemical or astronomical phenomena. The Science of Language, as established by the labours of the nineteenth century, combines the methods of the natural and the moral sciences. On one side it deals

with a purely natural evolution, on the other it studies
the workings of the human mind, which crosses the
stream of mechanical development and imperiously
turns it in directions which only the psychologist can
reduce to rule.

Perhaps I have said enough to suggest that the
Science of Language has a peculiar value as an
educating force. It may be fairly claimed that it
combines all the elements which are most necessary
for a really perfect educator. It is a science, and it
demands in the highest degree those methods of
exactness, of rigid investigation of facts and collection
of material, of precise and logical deduction, which we
associate with the physical sciences. But at the same
time it takes its material very largely from literary
sources ; and even where it deals with colloquial idiom
or non-literary dialects, the careful analysis of the
forms of speech cannot avoid the constant application
of principles which form the very basis of literary
composition. Our science therefore lies on both sides
of the frontier which divides the two great fields of
human study, and it is admirably adapted to correct
the narrowness which is often seen in those whose
training is purely literary or purely scientific.

The side of our science which presents itself to the
ordinary educated person is Etymology. No one can
fail to feel interested by a dip into a dictionary, which
tells us by what devious and lengthy paths words
have come to the meanings and forms they now show.
The dictionary of course only gives us results, which

may stimulate us to seek for processes to establish conclusions often paradoxical. When we are told that *Easter* is akin to the Latin *Aurora*, and *uncouth* to *ingens*, that *sooth*, (*pre*)*sent* and *suttee* all come from the participle of the verb "to be" as it shows itself in three cognate languages, with *onto*(*logy*) depending on a corresponding form in a fourth, we are easily convinced that the ways of words are peculiar. And when we trace the development of a word like *nice* back to the Latin *nescius*, "ignorant," or find in an old poem Christ described as a "silly knave," the words then meaning "holy boy," we can see that the laws by which words change their meaning are complex enough to give a science which examines them plenty of work to do.

The foundations of the science which changed etymology from mere random guessing into a sound process of reasoning were laid when, mainly through the labours of our great countryman, Sir William Jones, the Western world became possessed of the ancient language of India. That the classical languages of Greece and Rome were very closely connected had been always taken for granted : indeed their nearness to one another was greatly exaggerated. But that they formed only a part of a gigantic system of related languages, spoken by races scattered over the lands lying between India and Iceland, was never dreamt of till the obvious identity between the Sanskrit noun and verb systems and those of Greek and Latin was presented to the Western scholar's eye. It was Sir William Jones himself who first drew the momentous inference, in words which well deserve quoting : " The Sanskrit language, whatever may be its antiquity, is of wonderful structure ; more perfect than the Greek, more copious than the Latin, and more exquisitely refined than either, yet bearing to both of them a stronger affinity, both in the roots of verbs and in the forms of grammar, than could have been produced by accident ; so strong that no philologer could examine all the three without be-lieving them to have sprung from some common source which, perhaps, no longer exists. There is a similar reason, though not quite so forcible, for sup-posing that both the Gothic and the Celtic, though blended with a different idiom, had the same origin with the Sanskrit."   This brilliant discovery, declared in the year 1786, practically lies at the root of all linguistic science. Our science is not, of course, solely concerned with the languages of our own great family of speech, but the principles of the science have been built up exclusively through the study of this family, and no really scientific investigation of alien languages could possibly be carried on without the tools which we ultimately owe to the impulse given by the founder of the Royal Asiatic Society.

It was early in the nineteenth century when the English scholar's brilliant *aperçu* was taken up by the Germans, who developed it into a scientific fact, and have largely kept the study to themselves as a close preserve of German industry and thoroughness up to the present time. English genius has led the world in mathematics and physical science; while our literature for five hundred years has been without a rival among the literatures of Europe. In the study of the ancient classics we at least hold our own; but we do not seem to care to study the treasures of the English language, which in the hands of German students afford material for two periodicals exclusively devoted to them. And in the science of language we have only supplied occasional rivulets to swell the stream of progress; while our editors of classical texts are still too often content if in their etymological excursions they lag no more than twenty years behind the science of the day.

I must return from this digression, pleading in excuse of it the necessity of accounting in advance for the foreign names which will mark every step of the advance recorded in a brief sketch of a science born and matured within the nineteenth century. We begin then with the year 1816, thirty years after Sir William Jones's far-sighted announcement, when Franz Bopp published the first of a series of works in which he systematised the doctrine of the common origin of the languages of our family, and examined the history of their forms. His life-work may be said to have defined for us, practically on lines which we still follow, the limits and constituents of the Indo-germanic or Aryan family of languages. Before I go further, it may therefore be well to give some short description of the field as left by Bopp's labours, with very slight modification from later research. We

have eight main languages (apart from a few that are
only known by fragments), which descend from a
single approximately homogeneous original, long ago
lost. Arranged geographically as on the dial of a
clock, they will stand thus. (1) *Lithuanian*, still
spoken on the eastern shore of the Baltic; and
Slavonic, embracing Russian and other dialects of the
Slav nations. These, like the next two to be named,
are shown to be so closely akin that we must reckon
them as one branch rather than two. (2) *Iranian*, the
language of Persia; and *Indian*, by which we mean
Vedic and the classical Sanskrit, with its descendants
Hindi, Bengali, and others. The Indian and Iranian
branches are combined under the common title *Aryan*,
by which both peoples knew themselves in the earliest
times. (3) *Armenian*; and (4) *Albanian*—two less
important branches, whose original position on the
dial is not quite certain. We are now, from the
results of recent investigations, able to class these four
together as the *eastern* section of the family; the four
western branches will occupy the left-hand half of our
dial. These are (5) *Greek*, ancient and modern; (6)
Italic, including Latin and certain minor dialects of
ancient Italy, together with the Romance languages
of to-day, descendants of colloquial Latin; (7) *Keltic*[1],
which preserves a rather precarious vitality in Brittany,
Wales and Ireland, and even less than this in Scotland

---

[1] Italic and Keltic are so closely bound together by important
phonetic and morphological affinities that they are sometimes spoken
of as one branch.

and Man; and lastly (8) *Germanic*, the dominant language of all the lands of Western Europe which are not washed by the Mediterranean. We must allow at least the fourth quarter of our dial to this prolific member of the family, which at the top of the dial touches the first of the eastern branches, Lithuanian. A name has to be found which will conveniently represent the whole. German scholars insist on *Indo-Germanic*, a name combining the extreme east and extreme west of the language area. Far less cumbrous is the name *Aryan*, popularised in England by Max Müller, and plausibly supported by the etymology which traces the word in *Erin*—a fact which, if proved, would have gone far to show that the undivided people called themselves Aryans in prehistoric times. But since Aryan is a name undeniably appropriated by the ancient Indians and Iranians, it is safer to restrict it to the second of the eight main branches just described, and use for the whole family the title Indogermanic, which, if clumsy, is at any rate free from ambiguity.

Pursuing our historical order, we come next to the great name of Jacob Grimm. We all become familiar with that name in childhood through the great collection of folklore stories, in which the anthropologist and the small boy are equally at home. Later on, the sound of "Grimm's Law" forces itself on our attention, and the great principle therein laid down may very possibly be to this day the sole possession we hold in the realm of Comparative Philology. The

Law was enunciated in 1822, and may fairly be set
down to the account of the great scholar whose name
it bears, although the idea of it had been announced
before. Since it is obviously impossible in this lecture
even to sketch in the briefest manner the whole field
of Indogermanic philology, I shall probably lay out
my time to most advantage if I take up one or two
salient points and show their bearing on the principles
of the science as a whole. Grimm's Law is certainly
the best possible point from which to begin, for I may
fairly assume it to be generally known, and it is at
the same time of immense importance in the history
of linguistic study. Its importance is indeed utterly
out of proportion to the field which it immediately
affects. We who speak English can easily realise the
significance of a law which must be considered almost
every time when we seek Latin or Greek cognates for
words in our own language,—a law which in its further
development rules the relations between Dutch or
English and the literary language of Germany. But,
after all, there are other civilised languages besides
German, Dutch, or Norse, and even besides English,
and we may find ourselves asking whether Grimm's
Law would have quite the same perspective if we
were Frenchmen or Russians or Hindoos. Practically,
the answer would be yes. Grimm's Law is not merely
a convenience whereby we may scientifically equate
our word *brother* with the Latin *frater*, the Greek
φράτηρ, the Sanskrit *bhrātar*, and again the German
Bruder, or deny the identity of *call* with the Greek

καλῶ, for all their nearness of sound and meaning. It has proved in experience the great educator in the science of language. Its presence has perpetually reminded amateur etymologists—and it is astonishing how universally people feel themselves qualified to tackle an etymology, however innocent of special knowledge they may be—that there are laws governing the changes of human speech, which can only be set aside by the presence of other factors known to the expert alone. And even among experts, the wide extent of its operations and the sureness with which it works have done more than anything else, perhaps, to evolve the conviction that phonetic changes are exempt from mere caprice, and so to place our science upon the firm basis which it occupies to-day.

For the present I propose to develop the history of scientific method in terms of Grimm's Law, abandoning the strictly chronological order with which we began. How did this far-reaching change originate, and by what steps did it arrive at its present wonderful uniformity? In those fascinating *Lectures on the Science of Language*, by which the late Professor Max Müller did so much to popularise linguistic study in our country, an account is given which raises all at once the question of the nature of phonetic change. Practically it comes to this. The Germans found themselves no longer able to pronounce the difficult sounds *bh*, *dh* and *gh* which they had inherited from their Indogermanic forefathers, and (like several other members of the family) came to say *b*, *d* and *g* instead.

But this involved confusion with words which had a *b*, *d* or *g* already. Therefore, with a conscientiousness lacking in those other Indogermans, who did not mind the confusion, they replaced *b*, *d* and *g* by *p*, *t* and *k*. This, however, was thoughtless of them, for these sounds likewise were appropriated. Having committed themselves too far to go back, they had to bring in a new set of sounds, *f*, *th* and *h*, which accordingly took up the old *p*, *t* and *k*, and the "sound-shifting" was complete. We should have to postulate a somewhat similar process when, about a thousand years after the first sound-shifting, the High Germans started a second, by which the existing Germanic *b*, *p* and *f* were shifted on further to *p*, *pf* and *b*, with similar changes for the dentals and gutturals. You will probably anticipate the fatal objection against any such explanation. It postulates a *conscious* change, simultaneously adopted by a whole people, and the briefest reflexion will show that such things do not and cannot happen. Phonetic changes are not determined by committees. Speech is unconscious, except when we are trying to conform our pronunciation to that of our neighbours. The realisation of this point will prepare us for the study of the latest phase of enquiry upon which our science has entered. I cannot enter now on the solution of the interesting question as to the causes from which the "sound-shiftings" arose. Suffice it if I observe that no explanation will suit the phenomena of language which does not recognise the unconscious and independent character of the changes. Some may have changed by the imperfect efforts of natives to catch the pronunciation of foreigners. In others, an imperceptible variation beginning on one kind of sound alone, and presumably only under definite conditions—such as combination with other sounds, or appearance at the beginning or the end of a word—gradually spread till the change was complete for that set of sounds. Meanwhile another set would independently begin to suffer change, till after a few generations the process was accomplished without any of the speakers of the language knowing how far they had come.

I have not yet done with Grimm's Law, but for a few minutes I must relapse into history to show the background on which modern science is set forth. For this purpose we must pass over nearly half a century of laborious collection and ordering of facts, and neglect entirely the work of some of the greatest masters in Indogermanic philology. I pause on the names of Max Müller and Curtius, the more readily as they seem to represent the latest stage of science as conceived by many English scholars when obliged to venture on the unfamiliar ground of comparative philology. Both were champions of law and order in the realm of language, but their systems of law allowed room for a carnival, in which ordinary principles were suspended. Max Müller devoted himself to the special study of comparative mythology, and collected a large number of fairly similar names in Sanskrit and Greek, which he paraded as historically connected words. A complex fabric of primitive Indo-germanic mythology was thus constructed, mostly centring on manifestations of the Dawn-goddess. Alas! this pretty theory has long since vanished into air, into thin air, for hardly one of the innumerable equations will hold when examined by more rigid methods. Curtius attempted to hold the carnival under a semblance of restraint. He laid it down that when sounds began to become difficult, in the speech of any nation, they passed generally into some "regular" representative sound, but also "sporadically" into others. Thus the w sound in Greek, which we call digamma, "regularly" disappeared in the course of development, but "sporadically" metamorphosed itself into b, g, h, m, ph, r, o and u. Most of these were supported only by two or three examples, which were regarded as proof specimens on very arbitrary grounds. It was clear that although the realm of chance and caprice in language had been very greatly narrowed, there was still much to be done before anything like an exact science could emerge.

Between 1870 and 1880 certain brilliant discoveries were made which at one stroke reduced to order a large proportion of the irregularities left by earlier investigators into Indogermanic phonetics. The effect of such discoveries is rather like that of the discovery of Neptune in the realm of astronomy: serious irregularities traced down to some hitherto unsuspected new factor, the presence of which makes everything orderly, form a most impressive argument for the universal reign of law. It is fitting that among these discoveries should stand out an explanation of irregularities in the working of Grimm's Law. Verner's Law, as the new principle is called from its discoverer, deals with cases in which original *p, t* and *k*, instead of passing into *f, th* and *h* as Grimm's Law demands, become *b, d* and *g*. Verner showed that this depended on the position of the accent, and that the accent thus evidenced for the primitive Germanic was identical with that still preserved in Vedic Sanskrit and to some extent in Greek. This discovery gave a great impulse to the growing sense of regularity in language. At the same time it went far beyond Grimm's Law in the light it threw on the conditions of primeval Indogermanic speech, for the coincidence of the accent in the two most widely-severed branches of the family proved what the accent was in the original language from which both were descended. Verner's Law was accompanied by other discoveries which entirely transformed our conceptions of this original Indogermanic language. Schleicher, the great pioneer whose work marks the first decided advance from the standpoint of Bopp and Grimm, reconstructed the parent language as an exceedingly simple organism, with only three vowels, *a, i* and *u,* and consonants cut down to a small figure. The discoveries of later years, in which the name of Karl Brugmann holds the place of honour, turn this reconstruction into something far more complex. The simple vowels are extended to include *e* and *o* and others; by the side of *i* and *u*

stand *r, l, m* and *n* as sharing their power of becoming
vowels or consonants at will; the gutturals are turned
into three series instead of one, and on their behaviour
depends the allocation of any given dialect to the
Eastern or the Western side of the Indogermanic
family. In addition to this there is revealed a complicated system of stress and pitch accents. The
result is that if anyone learnt to speak the Indogermanic language as it stands to-day, he could not
possibly make himself understood by one who had
similarly learnt the language according to Schleicher.
Five for Schleicher was *kankan*, for us *pénqᵘe*[1]
(Western) or *pénqe* (Eastern): *horse* for him was
akwas, for us *échwos*[2], and so on. The difference may
be a useful warning if we are in any danger of regarding
our scientific reconstructions of the parent language as
the definite discovery of a dialect which was spoken at
one particular time in the dim and distant past. I shall
have to deal with this caution in the next lecture, in
which I shall try to show what help Language can give
us in unveiling the life and civilisation of those primeval
men from whom we are partially descended, and to

[1] The symbol *ŋ* represents our *ng*, the guttural nasal: the parasite
u (*u̯* is the consonantal *u*) is closely attached to the consonant—*peng-que*
(not *penk-we*) would represent the pronunciation.

[2] The "palatal *k* " (*k̑* in Brugmann's notation) was probably pronounced like the Scotch *ch* in *loch*. This will account for the Eastern
sh or *s*, and the Western *k* alike: the former change is paralleled by
the South German pronunciation of *nicht* as *nisht*, the latter by the
" *Lock* Lomond " which the steamer officials endure from so many
Southron lips in the tourist season.

whom we owe our speech. Meanwhile it will be enough to remind you that the forms which appear in scientific books, as due to the parent Indogermanic language, are only convenient formulae to show what we have learnt of the history of words extant in ancient or modern languages of our group. They *may* represent words actually spoken by prehistoric men, perhaps however at intervals of some centuries from one another. Or they may be as far from the words actually spoken as were Schleicher's reconstructions from those in vogue to-day ; for it can hardly be that this science will stand still in generations of research yet to come.

I pass on, then, to the brief enunciation and illustration of the principles of our science as we understand them now. What I have been saying will prepare you for the latest development of our theory. Exceptions to phonetic laws have been reduced enormously by the successive establishment of new laws covering every part of Indogermanic speech, and the natural result is that scholars have been drawn to go a step further and declare that phonetic laws, as such, admit of no exception. Since this bold declaration was first made by Leskien, in 1876, it has been furiously debated, and it may perhaps be questioned whether on grounds of theory alone it has been conclusively established. But some of the most contemptuous critics of the " Neo-grammarians," as they are called, have led the way in discovering new phonetic laws, and therefore in reducing further the

number of words which would have to be classed as
" irregular." Whether therefore we are or are not
prepared to assert as a matter of theory that there
cannot be irregularities in language caused by the
capricious action of phonetic law, we may certainly
use as a working principle the doctrine of the fixity of
law in human speech. For example, if anyone should
tell us that of course the Latin and Greek words
for *God, deus* and θεός, must have a common origin,
because they sound so nearly alike and have the same
meaning, we promptly deny the identity, because
phonetic laws stand in the way. A Greek *th* cannot
answer to a Latin *d* at the beginning of a word, and
we prove our point by citing a number of words in
which Greek *th* and Latin initial *f* stand in clear relation to one another, while we challenge the objector to
produce any other example in which a Latin *d* has
ousted the regular *f*. He declares that this is an
exception, and denies our right to assert that such
exceptions are inadmissible. It is quite unnecessary
for us to fall back on a general theory that Language
knows nothing of exceptions, acting always with the
precision of a law of nature. It is enough to say
that our opponent is bound to show cause why the
originals of our *deism* and *theism* must necessarily be
the same. Meaning and similarity of sound count
for nothing, for coincidences of the kind can be produced by the score. The Hebrew *kâphar* means *cover*,
but no one out of Bedlam thinks the identity a sufficient proof of our descent from the Lost Ten Tribes !

I proceed to show in what sense the dictum of the invariability of phonetic law is to be understood. I find it convenient to state the principle in the following form, to which I ask your special attention as covering the whole field in short compass.

"The same original sound cannot, in the same period of the same dialect, pass under the same conditions into two different sounds."

You will observe the four *sames* of this statement. Eliminate any one of them and you get what seems an irregularity. It will I think be helpful to give one or two illustrations under each of these heads.

First, then, "*the same original sound.*" Examples under this head may be supplied from all the novelties in linguistic discovery which I have been trying to sketch this morning. Take the English words *guest* (German *Gast*) and *warm*. The initials *g* and *w* are found alike in Sanskrit as *gh*, and it was formerly assumed that in such cases the Indogermanic sound was *gh*, which was differentiated later in Western languages into two sounds, the latter containing a *w*. We now know that the guttural in question was not the same in the two cases, the latter belonging to a series in which the *w* was strongly developed throughout the Western languages, and dropped in the Eastern. An illustration of a different kind may be seen in the English *-ough* words, which supply so powerful an argument to the advocates of phonetic spelling, and so strong an irritant to the foreigner trying to learn our language. In *plough* and *bough* alike the *ough* goes back to an Old English *oh*, while *dough* is from *dah*, and *Lough* is a Keltic word, coming under our third head below. Speaking generally, we may say that modern science tends to seek different originals when a wide-spread irregularity appears in the representation of what has been taken to be the same sound. To simplify the parent language, by reducing the number of sounds in it, is no longer felt to be obligatory. A very early language may be very complex in its sounds, and progress is at least as likely to weed out unnecessary sounds as to invent new ones.

We pass to our second heading, "*in the same period*." Phonetic laws must not be supposed to be permanent: they came into being slowly and unconsciously, and slowly and unconsciously they die away. It is always therefore vital that we should know of a given law at what period, as well as in what area, it worked. Grimm's Law will supply excellent examples. What we call the "first sound-shifting" ceased to act in the Germanic languages some centuries before Christ. It gave us words like *father*, where the *f* was undeniably sounded by our rude ancestors who roamed over Northern Europe before the time when Caesar was invading Britain. It had ceased to act long before the Saxons followed him thither. Consequently, when the Saxons borrowed Latin words like *strâta* they had no instinct leading them to change the *t* sound, and it has remained in the English word *street* for a thousand years. It would not have so remained had the Saxons been infected with the new tendency which in upper Germany was beginning to shift all these sounds afresh. The High Germans made *strâta* into *Strasse*, *pondus* into *Pfund*, etc.; but this tendency in its turn died away, and when Modern German borrows a Latin word like *praedico*, German *predige*, it leaves the *p* alone, just as English does in *preach*.

Thirdly, "*of the same dialect.*" The colossal irregularities of English are very largely due to dialect mixture. A thousand years ago English included many dialects, all with equal possibilities in the struggle for survival as the ultimate literary language of our country. The dialect which was spoken most typically not far west of Cambridgeshire[1] finally won the day; but words and forms from other dialects became imbedded in the standard language, so that to-day it presents a bewildering medley of inconsistencies. To a less extent, but still considerably, Latin similarly absorbed dialectic peculiarities. One example I may give, as a very pretty specimen of the way in which irregularities are cleared off in modern research. There are a number of Latin words in which an original *d* becomes *l*. *Lingua* is for *dingua*, as the English *tongue* will show when Grimm's Law has been applied. *Olere*, "to smell," is clearly connected with *odor*, "odour." *Larix* (our *larch*) is

[1] See Professor Skeat's interesting pamphlet on the place-names of Cambridgeshire (Cambridge Antiquarian Society).

akin to the English word *tree*. Proceeding on the assumption that dialect mixture was the probable cause of this irregularity, a distinguished philologist, Professor Conway, began to look for an Italian dialect in which all initial *d*s, or *d*s between vowels, became *l*. The remains of the dialect on which he fixed are extremely scanty. But it happens that Horace speaks of a small river called *Dĭgentia* which flowed past his country-house. Its modern name is *Licenza*, and Dr Conway showed that its name would be pronounced with the *l* by the Sabines, through whose district it flowed, but that when it emerged into Latin territory the older *d* would be heard. Modern Italian has here preserved the Sabine form, as Latin did in such words as I mentioned just now. It is therefore no longer necessary to say that "*d* remains *d* in Latin, but the rule is broken in a few words where *l* appears." On the contrary, *d* always remains *d* under these circumstances, and the *l* of *lingua* and *oleo* is simply due to borrowing from the Sabine dialect.

Finally, "*under the same conditions.*" A great feature of modern research has been the emphasis laid on the extent to which we change the pronunciation of our words in different surroundings. We say *right-e-ous, per-haps, sup-pose*, when we talk deliberately,—*richus, p'raps, s'pose*, when we are in a hurry. The *t* in *right* remains *t* unless there is a kind of *y* sound following it, as in the *righteous* of the educated man in a hurry, or the *right-you-are* (*ri-chu-are*) of the more slangy individual. An immense variety of differences are produced by the shifting of accent. The word *accent* itself, when a noun, would be correctly written *áksṇt*, the second syllable being reduced to a mere vocalic *n* by the stress on the first syllable; when a verb, *accént*, it has the full *en*. In general, we can never say positively that "the same original sound at the same period of the same dialect" will produce the same resultant sound in two different words, until we have examined into the effects of accentual conditions, neighbouring sounds, rapidity of pronunciation, and any other possible differences of condition which may affect the ultimate form of the words in question.

So much then for the changes in Language which are due exclusively to phonetic development. A few words should be added to describe the manner in which all these changes arise. It must be remembered that speech is transmitted entirely by the reproduction of sounds and words we have heard from others. An English infant, placed from the first in the care of Russians, Persians, or Zulus, would speak their language, and would not have the slightest inherited predilection in favour of English[1]. Speech is a joint function of the ears and the vocal organs, and both may fail to catch the sound correctly. So long as the variation is not serious enough to be noticed by those from whom he learns, the child will go on pronouncing

[1] Except that such a difference as that between the lips of Europeans and Zulus would possibly make some variation in the child's articulation of Zulu sounds.

in his own way; and by slow changes, accumulating from generation to generation, the dialect will progressively alter. But this is assuming that the community speaking the dialect is compact enough for its individuals to be in constant communication with each other. It is communication which preserves speech from change; and within such compact communities the rate at which pronunciation changes will depend entirely on their sensitiveness to variety in sound. If they are acute of ear, they will soon notice and check the variations introduced by the children who are learning to speak their tongue; if not, they will pass over the children's mispronunciations, and the language will change rapidly. Suppose however that the community is not compact, that people living at its extreme ends never meet. The result will be a gradual shading off of dialect from one end to the other; and if the area is sufficiently large, it may well be that the extremes are mutually unintelligible, though neighbours all along the line can understand each other easily. Now suppose that an agricultural people, scattered evenly over a large area, gradually change their habits and concentrate in towns. Clearly the result will be that each town will have a dialect of its own, to an extent depending on the amount of intercommunication with its neighbours; and when these communities become separated by migration beyond seas or rivers or mountains, barriers preventing intercourse, each dialect, pursuing its own development, will draw away from those which were once all but identical with it, till at last the limit of intelligibility is passed and a new language is established. Finally, there is the disturbing force of foreign languages to be reckoned with. A small body of warriors invades and conquers a large but weaker population. It generally follows that in a few generations the conquerors have been absorbed and speak the language of the conquered; but the invaders, learning the new language late in life, bring their own pronunciation, and many of their own words. I have no time to enlarge upon this subject of speech mixture, but if you follow up the science you will soon realise how great are its possibilities of influence upon the development of language.

Time forbids any adequate attempt to describe the immense province of speech which separates our science from the physical sciences and joins it to those in which the human mind is the object of study. On the purely phonetic side, as we have seen, language develops with almost machine-like regularity. But we perpetually find that phonetic laws are being crossed by forces which are almost as conscious and deliberate as the act of coining a new word, or applying an old one to a new meaning. These are the forces of *Analogy*, which assimilates the forms of words that are brought into frequent association with each other. The principle used to be known as "False Analogy," but there is really no reason thus to stigmatise a highly respectable and influential factor in the development of speech. We are under no sort of obligation to maintain the inherited forms of language when we can save our memories by bringing a minority of words into conformity with a majority. If we choose to say *sorry* instead of *sory* (from *sore*), we have introduced a "false" element, in that *sorry* and *sorrow* are not really akin. But since the words have come to be associated in meaning, it is more convenient that they should be brought near in form : the dictionary will keep us right on the etymology. Or, to take an example from the largest field of analogy's operations, when our ancestors gave up saying *raught* as the past tense of *reach*, was it a "false" analogy which made them realise that a past tense normally differs from a present by adding *d*? They discarded forms which once had a meaning in favour of forms which have a clear meaning still, and we can only regret the caprice which failed to insist on *teached* and *beseeched* as well, or, if that could not be, at least to make us keep the old forms and bring in *praught* to match them!

It is usual to classify the operations of analogy under the heads *formal* and *logical*. Formal analogy assimilates the declension or conjugation of words originally belonging to different categories. Material, or logical, analogy clears away variations no longer intelligible in the forms belonging to one word, after which formal analogy often steps in and uses the convenient innovation for the benefit of other words. A few examples will sufficiently illustrate the extent of these operations. Old English inherited from the Indogermanic period a system of vowel-gradation, originally the automatic result of accent. This dominated the forms of the past tense very largely, as it did those of the perfect in Greek. The first and third persons singular had the forms *sang*, *wrote*, *sat*, the second person singular and the whole plural showed *sung*, *writ*, *sit*. As late as Chaucer we still find *I wot*, *we witen*, in which same word Greek likewise presented the identical vowel distinction (οἶδα, ἴσμεν). Obviously the distinction served no useful purpose, and logical analogy cleared it away: later English said *we wot*, and Hellenistic Greek said οἴδαμεν. In French the regular forms evolved from the vulgar Latin *parábolo*, plural *parabolámus*, were (je) *parole*, (nous) *parlons*, those from *ámo*, *amámus*, were *aime*, *amons*: modern French has levelled these tenses, and only a few survivals like *j'ai*, *nous avons*, *je viens*, *nous venons*, intrude themselves upon the unwilling English schoolboy. Old English, like modern German, insisted on modifying the vowel of a word like *long* when the comparative suffix *er* was added, a necessity which no longer ("*lenger*," they would say) appeals to us. It was the same principle which made *feet* the plural of *foot*, and what would have now become *beek* the plural of *book*. From this last grammatical abortion formal analogy delivered us, by calling in the aid of the multitude of nouns which made their plural by the simple method of adding *s* or *es* to the singular. The same beneficent process destroyed a great number of highly interesting but highly inconvenient "strong perfects," in favour of the simple past in *d.* In some cases it worked in the opposite direction : common types like *tore* from *tear* and *bore* from *bear* naturally gave rise to *wore* for *weared*, and I have heard *scrope* and *brung* produced on the same principle by speakers more logical than educated.

The examples of Analogy which I have been describing are cases affecting a whole grammatical category. We may feel fairly certain that most of the new tense-formations or noun-cases, etc., which characterise the various dialects of the Indogermanic or other families of speech, owed their birth to this fertile principle. A single example, if it produces something convenient and " meets a felt want," as the advertisers say, is often quite enough to create a new class of forms. Take for example the suffix *-ise*, which in English, as in the Greek whence it was borrowed, can be added so freely to other words to make a new verb. It started in Greek mainly from an extremely small class of nouns with a stem in -ιδ-, from which a verb in -ίζω came by regular rule. But the form was so convenient that it spread at an extraordinary rate in Greek, was borrowed by Latin, passed on to French and finally to English, so that if a Mr MacAdam invented a new way of paving roads the language was ready to coin " macadamise," just as Greek could sum up in the opprobrious verb *Medise* the traitorous action of Greeks who helped the Medes in their attempt to destroy Greek liberty.

A very large class of analogy forms has nothing to do with grammatical categories, but consists of types which have affected a few words associated with them by likeness or contrast of meaning. In all languages such groups as numerals, colours, parts of the body, trees, points of the compass, etc., have influenced one another, especially in their endings. *Norther* loses its suffix to match *south*, but *northern* produces *southern*. The initial *f* of *four* is plausibly explained by association with *five*. Such associations will often start new suffixes, appropriated by use to a particular class of words. In Latin, presumably from one or two examples, a whole series of tree-names has arisen with a suffix *-snus* (as *al(s)nus, pi(ts)nus*). Names for groves of trees usually end in *-êtum*. In Latin and in Germanic the suffix *-wos* has become associated with colour words, simply because it happened to be common to two original colour adjectives, *blue* and *yellow*, Latin *flâvos* and *helvos*, whence it spread. Pairs like *health* and *weal, male* and *femel, hither* and *thather, either* and *nother*, assimilated one another and produced forms which could only reduce phonetics to chaos if the ever-present influence of analogy were not recognised. It is hardly going too far to say that whenever a single word shows serious difficulties in its formation, the first instinct of a modern philologist is to search for some twin word which could work upon it by analogy. Now in all this the question will naturally occur to you, " How did Language choose between altering A to match B and altering B to match A ? Granted that we should not be likely to say *I sat* but *we sit, I sang* but *we sung*, how is it that

we did not come to say in the past tense *I sit, I sung*?
Why not *mell* and *femel*, *other* and *nother*, *heal* and
weal?" To this question we can hardly give a general
answer, any more than we can to the allied question how
taught and *feet* resisted the processes which destroyed
raught and *beek*,—why *drownded* is vulgar, but *sounded*
correct, and so on. In many cases we can see a
reason. The form that proved the survivor shows
itself to have been in one way or another the fittest to
survive. It occurred in the larger number of forms,
or in those which were most in use—it avoided
an ambiguity—it was easier to pronounce—all
manner of such forces turned the scale in individual
instances. Sometimes the scale is only turned after
oscillations to and fro. Milton says *I sung* in the
seventeenth century, and Charles Wesley *he begun* in
the eighteenth ; and our existing *sang* and *began* may
have to yield their place, for all we know, before this
century is out. The systematisation of these mental
processes, by which Language has so much simplified
itself, will, I believe, afford plenty of work to the
student of Indogermanic philology for years to come,
the sphere of purely phonetic development leaving
us now, it would seem, little beyond details to work
upon.

This morning's sketch—and I need not point out
to you how absolutely sketchy a single lecture upon
so vast a subject must be—has indicated some of the
lines on which the modern languages have developed
throughout their long history. We have seen in

closing how they have been enabled to rid themselves of accumulated lumber, and evolve the combination of simplicity in form with wealth in resource which can fit them for the complex needs of modern life. Obviously the language which has most successfully shaken off what is useless, while keeping all that makes it expressive and concise, is likely to outrun its rivals in the struggle to become the leading language of the world. Heaven forbid that, with guests present from so many other nations than our own, I should attempt for one moment to argue which that victorious language is likely to be!

The principles which have this morning led us to the latest developments of speech will lead us also into its first beginnings. It will be my duty to-morrow, not indeed to venture on the thorny but fascinating problem of the Origin of Language, but to enquire what Language can teach us of our ancestors' lives in the distant past which, though recent when compared with man's earliest appearance on this planet, lies far behind all literature and all history. The investigation, even though it fail to open wide the door and reveal to us in clear and brilliant light the long vista of the past, will at least tell us something more of what Language is and what Language can do.

II. LANGUAGE AND PRIMITIVE
HISTORY.

"Linguistic Palaeontology," as the method of research which I am to describe this morning is usually
called, is one among many tools which we may use to
excavate the prehistoric past. Archaeology studies
its material relics. Geology offers to tell us under
certain conditions the dates to which they belong.
Botany and Zoology come in occasionally to pronounce upon arguments drawn from trees or animals
which are brought into association with primitive
man. Craniology measures the skulls of those who
were considerate enough to leave them behind, and
Ethnology pursues other methods of classifying their
racial characteristics. Anthropology and Folklore
investigate primitive man by studying his equally
primitive representatives among the savages of to-
day, and by following out through modern survivals
the history of customs and institutions, superstitions
and magic. The Science of Language, as we have
seen, can do something towards reconstructing the

speech and vocabulary of the parent Indogerman peoples, who lived ages before the dawn of history, and it is clear that this reconstructed vocabulary, if properly used, can tell us many facts about the life of these interesting forbears of ours. The methods I have described are of course allies, to be regarded as necessary to one another's efficiency, and on no account to be used exclusively or with exaggerated belief in their powers when standing alone.

There are scholars who seem to regard Language as almost entirely useless for this purpose. They press the weaknesses of Language as evidence till they persuade themselves that it is sheer waste of time to study Linguistic Palaeontology at all. As usual, the truth would seem to lie between two extremes. To reject the mass of evidence, the nature of which I am to describe, is surely scepticism gone mad. To imagine Language capable of proving what we ask of her, without help from sister sciences, is an equally foolish presumption. The truly scientific method is to examine most carefully the cautions with which the argument from language must be applied, and then to test every conclusion by evidence derived from other sources. Proceeding in this way we can hardly fail to get some trustworthy results.

Let us then note firstly the cautions to be observed in making our vocabulary of primitive speech, and secondly those which come in when we seek to use what we have made. Under the first head we note

that the presence of a word in two or more branches
of the Indogerman family is not conclusive for its
right to a place in the primitive vocabulary. It is
impossible to distinguish decisively between a case of
inheritance and a case of early borrowing in " culture
words," for the name naturally spreads with the thing
when a new addition is made to the possessions of a
people. For instance, the word *fish*, which is common
to the Italians, Kelts, and Germans, but not extant else-
where, may have arisen in one of these contiguous
peoples and spread to the other two: Language
perhaps does not deny, but it assuredly does not
encourage the idea that a prehistoric Izaak Walton
taught his art to the undivided Indogermans. We
can only feel confident when a word is found in
branches widely separated in geographical position,
and of course the more there are of them the safer
we feel. On the other hand, the absence of a word
from many branches is not conclusive evidence
against it, for the loss of old words is a perpetual
phenomenon in all languages. The primitive words
son[1] and *daughter* have disappeared in Latin, *father*
and *mother* in Gothic, and *sister* has so far disappeared
from Greek that only an old lexicon gives evidence
for its former existence. We can ourselves watch the
superseding of *hound* by the foreign importation
"dog," and many similar cases may be observed.

---

[1] Throughout this lecture, where an English word is thus printed in
italics, it stands for the Indogermanic word from which it is directly
descended: thus *son* for *sūnús*, *mother* for *mātēr*, etc.

Moreover the absence of a common name does not prove the absence of the thing. The Indogermans had no common word for "one," though they had numerals from *two* up to *hundred*, no word for "hand," though *foot* is found everywhere. We can hardly infer that their physical and mental equipment was so deficient as the argument from silence would suggest in these cases. Besides this we have to remember that care is needed before we set down a word as absent from any particular language. Gothic comes down to us only in the Biblical version of Wulfila, the important Umbrian dialect of Italy only in some scanty ritual tablets. Clearly we can only argue absence in such cases when a missing old word is very frequently replaced by another, as we saw just now happened to *father* and *mother* in Gothic. Even in Greek, with its enormous extant literature, we find the dictionary enlarged whenever a new work is unearthed, or a new batch of inscriptions or papyri.

Then in using our vocabulary we must take note of the warnings received from "Semantics," the study of the meanings of words. The Latin cognate of *beech* agrees with the English, but the Greek means "oak"; the Greek answering to *tree* also means "oak," while in some languages it means "fir" or "pine." Nor must we be hasty in drawing conclusions from the existence of words with ascertained meanings and indubitable authority. Early philologists drew very rosy pictures of home life in the

primeval age on the strength of their etymologies—
father meant "protector" and *daughter* "milkmaid."
In these days we prefer not to dogmatise about the
etymology of words which come down to us entire
from the earliest period. Then, to take another kind
of example, the cognates of the Latin *equos*, which
are found in almost every main language, and always
with the meaning "horse," have been regarded as
proof that the Indogermans tamed and used the horse
for agriculture or war. The least thought will show
that the mere word proves nothing but their familiarity
with it and its being sufficiently important to them
to be worth naming. A prehistoric cowboy on horse-
back cannot be deduced from language alone, and for
all the linguist can tell to the contrary, the interest of
the Indogerman in the quadruped may have been
purely culinary.

In the former lecture I gave some account of the
main branches of the Indogermanic family, as arranged according to language. It is remarkable that
from the earliest dawn of history the six principal
languages belong to races arranged relatively as we
see them now. Indian and Iranian, Slavonic and
Lithuanian, the two main branches of the east
Indogermanic languages, are found still in their
relative position, with Germanic, Keltic, Italic, and
Greek following in this order down the western side
of the map. If we squeeze them all together, leaving
the Lithuanians and Germans near the shores of the
Baltic, and the rest on lines running to the south-east

and south-west or south respectively, only shorter than they were before, we shall obtain a very probable position for the races speaking those languages at the dawn of history.

At this point the researches of archaeologists and historians come in to show us that the great north European race, associated especially with the Keltic and Germanic languages, in the prehistoric period sent out successive swarms of sturdy invaders who established themselves as a conquering caste in various southern lands. Their tall stature, yellow or sandy hair and blue eyes contrasted strongly with the features of the short, dark-haired and swarthy races which inhabited the shores of the Mediterranean. In his brilliant book on *The Early Age of Greece* Professor Ridgeway has made it highly probable that Homer's Achaeans belonged to this conquering northern race, before whom the indigenous " Pelasgians," represented most faithfully by the Athenians and Ionians generally, were forced to bow. Traces of northern origin remain in Greek traditions of places of ceaseless sunshine, and places of perpetual darkness where the air was full of wool—of floating rocks (icebergs?) that crashed together over the sea—of the quest of the "golden-horned hind," which can only be the reindeer. Baltic amber has been found in Greek tombs. The study of manners and customs and beliefs tells the same tale. It is remarkable also that some conspicuous heroes of the *Iliad* and *Odyssey* have names which cannot be accounted for as Greek, whereas native Greek names are almost always transparent in their etymology. It is interesting to add to Professor Ridgeway's point an unconscious confirmation from the great philologist August Fick, who found a congener for *Achilles* in the old German name *Agilulfs*. Dr Ridgeway believes that the same origin can be asserted for the sturdy Sabine race, who formed the "patrician" nucleus of the early population of Rome, and whose kindred in later ages made so brave a struggle for independence against the growing power of the great city. We can probably trace the same strain further east. Cyrus and his victorious Persians present many of the characteristics which we note in the patricians of Rome and the Achaeans of Greece, and in all these we have the same subsequent history: a comparatively small host of warriors, greatly superior in physique and equipment, easily conquers a weaker population, and in a few generations loses most of its distinctive features by intermarriage with the indigenous race. There are traces still remaining of these kinsfolk of our own who in distant ages overran the rich lands of southern Europe and western Asia, inhabited by races physically weaker but more intellectual than themselves. In India the rigid preservation of caste barriers enables observers still to note the decidedly northern physiognomy of some representatives of ancient royal houses. And among the Ossetes, an Iranian-speaking folk in the centre of the Caucasus, modern travellers have been curiously agreed in noting customs strongly reminding them of Germany.

Between these two[1] widely different races we shall find immense differences of customs and culture. The question will of course be asked, which of the two races represents the primitive Indogermanic people? It may be doubted whether we shall ever be able to answer such a question. If we must choose, we can hardly doubt that the northern race has the prior claim, and the affinities between Indogermanic and Finnish speech, accepted as proved by the high authority of Dr Sweet, undeniably make in this direction. On the same side stands Dr Ridgeway's proof that the Achaeans brought with them the worship of Zeus, an unquestionably Indogerman deity, while the indigenous Poseidon bears a name which has so far defied analysis. But, on the other hand, the non-Achaean Greek and the non-Sabine Latin only differ dialectically from the language of the invaders, so far as we can disentangle them. The same conditions seem to prevail in Media, where the non-Aryan[2] population cannot be shown to have spoken a language radically different from that of

[1] The blond northern race is here spoken of for convenience as one. But the conquerors of southern Europe included not only long-headed but also short-headed men, who lived in great numbers in south Germany; so that there were really two different stocks among them. So Professor Ridgeway informs me.

[2] I am of course using the term Aryan in its strict sense, as the self-chosen name of the family speaking the closely-related Indian and Iranian languages.

their Aryan conquerors. It must not be forgotten
that race and language cannot be treated as necessarily going together. Two totally distinct races
may very well speak closely related languages, and
the difference of speech may be the result of the
fact that one race learnt the language as a foreign
idiom. But if the Mediterranean race did learn their
language from the peoples of the North, it must have
been in a prehistoric period at which it is absolutely
impossible for us to arrive with our present methods.
The period of this assumed process antedates the
dialectic division between the eastern and western
Indogermanic languages, a division which goes back
as far as our knowledge can take us. The typically
northern Keltic and Germanic lie in this respect on
the same side as the typically Mediterranean Latin
and "Pelasgian" Greek. It is better therefore to
acquiesce in our ignorance, and say that both races
spoke Indogermanic at the very earliest period to
which our science can approach.

And where did these primitive people live?
"Somewhere in Asia" was the answer universally
given till comparatively lately. Whether the Book
of Genesis was supposed to demand this, or whether
it resulted from a general idea of the fitness of things,
is rather hard to say. In 1851 R. G. Latham—of
whom as in private duty bound I must chronicle that
he was a Fellow of King's College, Cambridge—pro-
pounded the revolutionary view that the home was
to be found in Europe. His reasons centred on the

antecedent probability that the dog would wag the tail and not the tail wag the dog. He was scoffed at as a " crack-brained Englishman" by the superior Germans. But the whirligig of time brings its revenges, and there is hardly a German now with a reputation to lose who does not hold with Latham. There is one very interesting exception, that great philologist Johannes Schmidt, recently deceased, who invented an argument for the Asiatic hypothesis, insufficient indeed to bear the weight he laid upon it, but well worth respectful consideration. He pointed out that there were in European languages considerable traces of a sexagesimal system of numeration crossing the decimal—the peculiar formation of our own *eleven* and *twelve*, and the Germanic "long hundred," for 120, will serve as examples,—and he argued that this must be due to a very early contact with the Babylonians[1], with whom 60 was the pivot of the numeral system. It seems clear that we should call our European peculiarity duodecimal rather than sexagesimal, and that other causes must be accepted

---

[1] Schmidt throws in other supposed borrowings from Babylonian. The most plausible of these is the Greek πέλεκυς " axe," Sanskrit *paraçus*, compared with Assyrian *pilaqqu*. I cannot feel satisfied with his account of the relation between the Assyrian *q* and the Sanskrit *sh* sound, and I think this is to be added to the remarkably large category of purely accidental similarities. πέλεκυς and *paraçus* will suit the root *pelek̂* (Latin *plecto*, our *flay*), and the original meaning may have been a knife for cutting hides. Schmidt's doctrine has received a serious blow from the other side in Dr Ridgeway's proof that the sexagesimal system was of quite recent date in Babylonia.

for its appearance than that which Schmidt demanded, but we may still admire the ingenuity of the only serious argument which recent years have brought to the support of a theory once taken for granted as an axiom.

We have no time to indicate the various lines of evidence which converge on northern Europe as the most probable centre of radiation for the emigrations of prehistoric ages. It must be carefully noted that we only seek to determine the home of the Indogermans at the latest period at which they were speaking mutually intelligible language. Of their earlier home and culture Language can naturally tell us nothing whatever; and if other methods of research decide that our forefathers ultimately started from Asia or from the North Pole, our science cannot say no. For the period to which Language leads us, a northern origin seems at least favoured by the prominence of winter and cold. *Snow* is certainly Indogermanic, and possibly *ice*[1] as well, while winter was known by the name found in the Latin *hiemps* and the Sanskrit *Himâ*laya ("abode of snow"). Spring also (Latin *ver*) was a very well-marked season. An argument has been found in the names of trees which are shown by language to have been known to the Indogermans. The oak and the pine, and less

[1] The Zend *isi*, if we might slightly alter the sibilant in the one place where it occurs, suits the Germanic *ice* very well, and an attestation from Aryan and Germanic means more than one from any other two Indogermanic languages, as these are the farthest apart.

conspicuously the willow and the birch, are decisively proved to have existed in the primitive period, and these four are said not to be found together outside Europe[1]. The argument is complicated by the extraordinary propensity of the tree-names to change their meaning. When people migrated into a region where a particular tree was rare or absent, they would use its name for "tree" in general, or for some other tree. Thus in Italy *fraxinus*, the cognate of our *birch*, is used to denote the ash. I may mention two examples of the methods by which we may fix the original meaning of these words. *Tree* means "oak" in Greek and Keltic, "wood" or "tree" in Germanic and Albanian, "larch" in Latin. The cognate *tar*, with one of similar meaning in Lithuanian, decides us for a resinous tree, presumably the pine, as the original. *Fir* means "oak" in Latin (*quercus*), a kind of fig-tree in Sanskrit, and it has indeterminate derivatives in Keltic, Gothic, Lithuanian, etc. But a word for the Thunder-god derived from it argues for "oak" as the earliest meaning, for the oak-tree and the thunder were old associates, as we shall see later.

Pursuing our enquiry, we find that the Indogermans were familiar with the sea (*mere*, Latin *mare*). The older investigators were most unwarrantably sceptical on this point. Holding as they did an exaggerated view of the importance of the Aryan

---

[1] So Hirt, an able philologist. But an excellent botanist tells me he is wrong. How necessary it is to "verify our references"!

branch in all such enquiries, they denied Indogerman antiquity to words which were not to be found in Indian or Iranian languages. Since Aryan is now found to be closely united to its neighbours, the Slavonic on one side and the Armenian on the other, we cannot lay the same stress on the absence of Aryan attestation. The word *mere* has in its form strong witness to its high antiquity; and, the Aryan migration being entirely inland, they may easily have lost the word before they reached the Caspian or other great sheet of water. I cannot stay to argue the case for the Baltic as the sea of the Indogermans. I need only point out that it meets all the conditions, so long as we do not insist on the immediate contact of the whole people with the seaboard, but conceive of them as spreading inland to the south-east and south-west in two streams as described already. That the converging point on the Baltic is still the home of the Lithuanians is itself no mean argument, for this people retains to the present day a most disproportionate amount of primitive features in its language, which is at once accounted for if we take them to be descendants of the original folk occupying still the original home. The region of our hypothesis still harbours the wolf and the bear, beasts thoroughly familiar to the primitive people, who knew nothing (so far as language can tell us) of the Asiatic elephant or tiger. There are bees to supply honey for making *mead*, on which I fear the primitive Indogerman had learnt to make himself drunk to an extent quite worthy of his noble descendants, the heirs of all the intervening ages. Gigantic trees were there to be felled and hollowed by fire to make the "dug-outs" in which they navigated the streams; and in the vast and awesome woods we can picture them worshipping *Diêus Perqûnos*, Zeus of the oak, with rites not greatly differing from those of the Druids in historical times.

From this centre we may conceive the Indo-germans spreading as their numbers grew, and their dialects gradually developing in the way I tried to describe in the former lecture. It would naturally happen that some of the tribes thus formed would remain in contact with one another long after they had ceased to be in touch with their other kin, so that new culture characteristics and new terms to describe them spread throughout a limited area without affecting those who had detached themselves before these new departures took place. A good example may be found in the evidence mentioned earlier in this lecture, connecting the common culture of the Italians, Kelts, and Germans with the period of the Swiss Lake-dwellers, who differ from the earlier Indogermans by the prominence of fish in their diet[1].

---

[1] I should remark here that Professor Ridgeway, speaking as an archaeologist, pronounces primitive man, wherever found, largely a fish-eater. I am dealing only with the evidence of language, and if the archaeologists press this point we must of course assume either (1) that *fish* (Latin *piscis*, Old Irish *iasc*) was lost in the other five main

It remains for us to ask what light our science can cast on the arts and accomplishments, the family life and the religion of this primitive people. It is usual to gauge the progress of nations in early stages of development by the extent of their acquaintance with metals. The test does not pretend to be complete, for it is obvious that a people still in the Stone Age may be more advanced and more civilised than one which has learnt something of the use of metals. But practically the test is found quite good enough for its purpose, and it is therefore the best course for us to ask first what was the condition of the Indogermans in this respect. We find that there is fairly decisive evidence that they were acquainted with copper, which they knew by two names, one the ultimate origin of our word *iron*, the other possibly a derivative from the adjective *red*. The only other metal they could have known is gold, which like copper is often found on the surface pure. The Germans, Letts and Slavs—contiguous peoples, be it noted—must have learnt its use very early, and agreed to name it by its present name, derived from the root of *yellow*. Some rather tempting Sanskrit evidence for this word has been alleged, but it is

Indogerman dialects, especially by those whose migrations took them across the steppes, or to seas where the fish were unappetising,—or (2) that the Indogermans, as in the case of " one " and " hand " (p. 33), possessed the thing but not the name in common. It seems to me, however, at least a striking coincidence that *fish* belongs exclusively to these three contiguous peoples, who may so well have radiated from the Lake-dwellers' area.

hardly to be relied upon ; and, if it were, it only
involves extending the chain of contiguous tribes
possessing the name one more link to the east. At
first sight, the case for silver appears stronger, inas-
much as Aryans, Armenians, Italians and Kelts use
the same word, while Greek has the same root with
the suffix changed. But on further examination we
find that it only involves the coincident use of a word
for "white," to which not very recondite piece of
nomenclature the great wits of various tribes may
well have jumped independently. For other metals
no semblance of a case can be made out. It will be
obvious that the absence of a common name for the
various metals is in this case a very serious argument,
for though a word for "hand" may as we have seen
be missing without our drawing the inference we
draw here, we have the best possible evidence from
archaeology that the Indogermans *did* possess hands,
evidence which is conspicuous by its absence in the
case of the metals. We conclude that the Indogermans were in the Neolithic stage of culture,
slightly modified by their use of copper. This fact
incidentally supports our decision against the Asiatic
home ; for the Semites, while still one undivided
people, knew gold, silver and copper, and it is very
hard to believe that the Indogermans would have
remained ignorant of all but copper, had they started
from a country comparatively near the Semite home,
especially if, as Schmidt's theory demands, they had
actual contact with the Semites in a very early period.

We soon find that *dulce domum* was an idea familiar to the earliest Indogermans, for *domus* (our *timber*, German *Zimmer*) is a word found everywhere. It seems moreover to connote "home" as well as "house," for it is used to describe the household as well as the dwelling, and the "house-master" and "house-mistress" (cf. the Greek word from which we get our *despot*) took their names from it. We must leave the archaeologists the last word as to the character of the house. Language supports the assumption that there was one room specially named from the central hearth, with a large opening in the roof above to let the smoke escape. *Oven* and *cook* are both primitive words, but we must not let our ideas approach too near the processes of a modern kitchener; an earthen pot hung from three sticks over the fire is perhaps as likely as anything. The fact that the *wagon* was known, with axle and wheels presumably in one piece, has suggested that the Indogermans were gipsies, differing from their modern descendants only in the inferior finish of their caravan. But there is no necessary connexion, and wagons originally used for living in may well have been retained for agricultural use. That agriculture was practised, probably side by side with the keeping of flocks and herds, for which *cow*, *steer* and *ewe* are primitive words, seems certainly established. *Corn*, and the German *Gerste*, are well-attested primitive words, and there are too many others of the kind to make it probable that the Indogermans only collected wild-grass seeds. The words *quern* and *mill* are equally old, and so are the verbs *ear* and *sow*, and probably the name of the finished article, *loaf.* The names for "plough" often tell their own tale by their connexion with words meaning "branch." The older scholars' hesitation to accept agriculture as Indo-germanic arose largely from the fact that most of these words are either absent or have become colour-less ("move," "go," and the like) in the Aryan languages. But there is no reason why we should allow Aryan a decisive weight which we should never think of granting to any other single branch of the family; and when we have recognised that the Aryans' migration to their present homes took them across the steppes we have at once the sufficient reason for their losing words denoting processes of agriculture, which could be rarely applied.

It is naturally impossible here to attempt a com-plete sketch of the life of this prehistoric people. I might mention that they had discovered arts to which the words *weave* and *sew* attached themselves : of course they would be in the most elementary stage of development. What gives us a yet higher idea of their progress is the apparent fact that they achieved a very near approximation to the length of the solar year. (*Year*, like *month*, is primitive, but probably meant "spring," as does sometimes its Greek cognate from which comes the word "hour.") Twelve lunar months, 354 days, seem to have been the first approxi-mation, which would soon be found to be too short.

A " little year " of twelve days brought the year to what is practically correct. We find these twelve days kept with special ceremonial at the two extremes of the Indogermanic area ; and each day up to " Twelfth Night " was supposed to forecast the weather of a corresponding month in the year following.

The family conditions of the Indogermans claim our attention before we begin to describe their religion, the last topic on which we shall have time to dwell. The very large number of relationship words strikes every observer. *Father, mother, son, daughter, brother, sister,* are our share in the primitive inheritance ; and to these may be added words for grandson and granddaughter, son's wife, husband's father and mother, husband's brother and sister (?), and perhaps grandfather, stepmother, uncle, son-in-law, brothers' wives, sisters' husbands. The relationships seem mostly to be on the male side, but there are possible survivals of a " matriarchate," and in any case the position of women seems to have been passably good for so early a stage of civilisation. There was a great difference between the North European and the Mediterranean races in this respect. Everyone notices the extraordinary contrast between the position of women at Athens, in the age of her greatest fame, and that of the Homeric women, some six centuries earlier. The apparent degeneration is explained at once by Professor Ridgeway's theory, for the Achaean women are in just the same social condition as those of ancient Germany, as described by Tacitus, which is also reflected in the life of the patrician matrons at Rome. It was not from the northern invaders that the slavery of women in India came. At the same time it is suggestive that *widow* is a primitive word, while there is none to describe the widower: we may probably infer that the widow was at any rate not re-married.

The clan was apparently the highest political unit. The wife would be brought in by purchase from another clan: the word *wed* is specially associated with this purchase-money. The slaying of a member of the clan—originally denoted in Italy by the word *parricide* (which only popular etymology connected with *pater*)—imposed a special obligation on the survivors. The northern race were content to exact a wergild from the homicide or his clan; but the Mediterranean people, believing as they did that the shed blood cried from the ground, and that the unsatisfied spirit was always near the living and powerful to harm, insisted on blood revenge, nor has the practice died out in our own day.

We have come to a point at which it is natural to go on to the investigation of Indogermanic religion. The wide differences of view which have been held on this subject suggest that a solution is most likely to be found on the lines of Professor Ridgeway's fruitful theory. There are plentiful traces of ancestor-worship. The Romans had their *Manes*, and the Greeks never lost their deep-seated conviction that the souls of the dead dwelt in or near their tombs,

mighty to help or hurt those whose most sacred
duty was to care for their ancestors' graves, and give
the shades a momentary taste of renewed life by
drink-offerings of blood poured through a little
opening into the tomb. So indestructible was this
belief, that in the island of Thera we find a number
of Christian tombs with the Greek inscription "The
angel of so-and-so": the old pagan ancestor-spirit
had a new lease of life when christened as a guardian
angel. On the other hand we find that the Achaeans
burnt their dead, and believed that the spirit after the
burning flew away to the Isles of the Blest, never to
return. The mixture of these two contrary ideas
produced inextricable confusion in the eschatology
of the later Greeks; but among the kindred of the
Achaeans in Northern Europe we find their ideas in
their original purity. There is moreover from all
quarters evidence of nature-worship as the creed
of original speakers of Indogermanic languages.
Classical writers portray for us the religion of the
ancient Germans and Gauls and Persians, and the
portraits agree in the prominence assigned to the sun
and moon, and to the associated worship of heaven
and earth, which latter were regarded as father and
mother of all. These ideas are reflected in the one
divine name which is common to many branches of
the Indogermanic family. The Greek *Zeus*, the
Italian *Jove*, the Germanic deity whose name we
preserve in *Tues*-day, answer to the old Vedic
Dyaus, whose worship evidently failed to take

root among the peoples of India conquered by the northern warriors, for even in the earliest Vedas he is a name and little more. I am myself tempted to conjecture that when Herodotus tells us of the Persian popular faith, and observes that they "called the whole vault of heaven Zeus," he was not merely using the familiar name of the Greek supreme deity, to describe the supreme deity of another people, but reproducing the very word he had heard in Persia[1]. Closely akin to this name is the general word for God, whence the Latin *deus* and *divinus* descend[2]. The name presumably means "shining," and fits the nature deity of the northern race, as completely as the Greek θεός, if its congener is really to be sought in Lithuanian and German words for "ghost" or "spirit," fits the ancestor-worship of the Mediterranean peoples. It is impossible for us to enter further here upon the features which language and archaeology combine to authenticate for early times. One interesting point may be noted with reference to the

[1] Herod. I. 131 τὸν κύκλον πάντα τοῦ οὐρανοῦ Δία καλέοντες. The old word for "heaven" probably survives in one passage of the Avesta; and, as the present writer has tried to show, in a forthcoming article on the religion of Persia, the common people probably kept up the old nature-worship long after the court had adopted the reform connected with the great name of Zoroaster. If the name Dyaus still survived, a Greek could only suppose it Zeus, especially if he heard it in the accusative case.

[2] And, according to one excellent authority, *Tues*(day), which would thus become in its origin a common and not a proper noun. But the older view cannot be regarded as conclusively ruled out by the phonetic objection raised against it.

god who seems clearly marked out as supreme, at any rate among the northern folk. It may be regarded as fairly certain that Diêus had not only the title "Father" but the further appellative *Perqûnos*, "of the Oak." The latter name has become a title of a rain or thunder god among the Vedic Indians (probably), the Norwegians—who applied it to the mother of Thor—and the Lithuanians, while among the Albanians it denotes "God" or "heaven." We have from Homer evidence of a sacred oak in Dodona, where special priests of Zeus ministered, "with unwashen feet and making their bed on the ground"—instances of the holiness of dirt which may be abundantly paralleled in the Fakirs of Hinduism and other religions. The northern cult of Zeus was, on Dr Ridgeway's theory, brought with them by the invading Achaeans through Epirus to Greece proper, and the shrine of Dodona preserves this worship in its last stage before it was fused and harmonised with the cult of Poseidon and other deities which existed in Greece before the invasion. The combination of Sky and Oak is not an obvious one to our minds, but to the primitive man the connexion was easy. The Sky-god sent the lightning which blasted the Oak, the chief of trees, and presumably the most abundant in the region where the cult arose. A peculiar sanctity was always, even in much later ages, attached to objects and persons struck by lightning, and the blasted oak was considered to be the special abode of the Sky-god who had thus come to his own. Apart from the sanctity of the oak, the fact that words for "acorn" are widely attested, and have primitive appearance, would seem to suggest that the tree provided food for man as well as beast. It is interesting to note how the "rain from heaven and fruitful seasons," declared by St Paul to be God's witness of Himself to the heathen world, produced among the remote ancestors of those to whom he spoke a cult of the sky that gave rain and the tree that bore fruit. And "the times of that ignorance God overlooked," well pleased—we are encouraged to believe—that even by the imperfect nature-worship of the "Sky Father" He had led His children to know that they were "His offspring."

The other strain of primitive religion, the ancestor-worship, is hardly supported at all by evidence from language. The nearest approach to a common word for "spirit" is seen in the cognates of the Greek *theos*, already noticed[1]. The evidence is decidedly less satisfactory than that which proves nature-worship. Nearly all the Indogermanic peoples, however, seem to have practised this cult, even though they may not have used common words for it. The fusion of the two conceptions of religion may well be as old as the spread of the common language over two very distinct races, and in this case the science of language cannot come to the aid of history. It will remain only a theory, made plausible rather by archaeology and history than by linguistic evidence, that ancestor-

[1] See Schrader, *Reallexikon*, p. 28.

worship was originally the religion of the Mediterranean people, and filtered northwards just as the worship of Diêus Perqûnos spread over the south. The two strains met conspicuously in the Greek religion, and very evidently played their part in preparing the Greek mind for its ultimate work in the propagation of a world religion.

So must end this brief and fragmentary introduction to a fascinating study. That many phases of primitive Indogermanic life, on which the evidence of speech is attainable, have been entirely passed over, while those that are not passed over have only a few leading features indicated, is obvious enough, and belongs to the conditions under which the present task is undertaken. But I hope it will be found that the selections given will whet the appetite for more, and that even this meagre sketch will do something to show how wide and how suggestive a study lies behind the words we unthinkingly use in daily life.

BIBLIOGRAPHY.

A short list of books on the subjects sketched in these lectures, available for English readers, may be found useful. Comparatively few of them will appeal to the general reader, but the student will find them within his grasp if he has a fair acquaintance with the structure of Latin and Greek and English. The books are classified, the easiest being put first in each section, with a few notes on each.

A. THE STUDY OF LANGUAGE (GENERAL).

Sweet, H.—*The History of Language.* (Temple Primers.) Dent, 1899.

Though only a primer, this little book contains a large amount of original matter, especially on the relations of the Finnish and other languages to the Indogermanic family.

Strong, Logeman and Wheeler.—*Introduction to the Study of the History of Language.* Longman, 1891.

An adaptation of the difficult, but most important, work by H. Paul, on *Principles of Language.* (The English *translation* of this latter work, by Strong, is not recommended.)

Whitney, W. D.—*Life and Growth of Language.* (Internat. Science Series.)   King, 1875.

Due allowance must of course be made for the immense development of the subject since the publication of this work ; but the great American scholar's teaching in many ways cannot go out of date.

Oertel, H.—*Lectures on the Study of Language.* Arnold, 1901.

By far the best general account of the subject, acute, correct, and original.   Like the last, this book is due to an American scholar.

Giles, P.—"Philology" (in new Supplement to *Encyclopaedia Britannica*).   See under C.

B.   ETYMOLOGY.

Skeat, W. W.—*Primer of English Etymology.*   Clarendon Press, 1892.

  ,,   ,,   —*Principles of English Etymology.*   2 vols. Clarendon Press, 1891, 1892.

  ,,   ,,   —*Etymological Dictionary of the English Language.*   3rd ed.   Clarendon Press, 1898.

  ,,   ,,   —*Concise* do.   Latest edition (rewritten), 1901.

For practical use this last supersedes everything else, containing as it does the matured results of many years' work by the leading English authority on Middle English.

Kluge, F., and Lutz, F.—*English Etymology;* a select glossary. Blackie and Son, 1899.

A much smaller book than Skeat's *Concise Dictionary*, but exceedingly sound and reliable.

Taylor, I.—*Names and their Histories.* Rivingtons, 1896.

A glossary of place-names, selected from various countries, with an introduction and appendices.

C. MEANINGS OF WORDS.

BRÉAL, M.—*Semantics.* Heinemann, 1900.

Practically a first attempt to deal with the science of meanings systematically. Dr J. P. Postgate adds some valuable discussions to the English edition.

Murray and Bradley. — *The New English Dictionary.* Clarendon Press (in progress).

This colossal work traces the history of every English word by quotations reaching back to its earliest appearance: the etymology is also examined. It is of course the final court of appeal in all matters concerning English words, no other dictionary pretending to cover more than a fraction of the ground here occupied.

Giles, P.—" Philology" (in new Supplement to *Encyclopaedia Britannica*).

This article is mentioned here specially because there is so little literature as yet dealing with the general principles of Semantics: it is however to be consulted on most of the subjects referred to in this little book. See also Mr Giles's article, *Writing*, in the same Supplement.

D. INDOGERMANIC LANGUAGES.

1. *General.*

Brugmann, K.—*Elements of the Comparative Grammar of the Indogermanic Languages.* 4 vols. and Index (a 5th vol.). Trübner, 1886–1897.

This encyclopaedic work, translated by Wright, Conway and Rouse, is the thesaurus of the results of the new philology, covering the phenomena of the eight main branches of the Indogermanic family in their older developments. The first volume, dealing with phonology, is superseded by the new German edition (1897); the second part, by Prof. Delbrück, which treats the Comparative Syntax on similar lines, is unfortunately not translated. Prof. Brugmann has been described above (p. 13) as the great pioneer of the new school, and the learning, clearness, and penetration visible throughout his work are extraordinary. He is now publishing (in German) an abridgement of it.

2. *Classical.*

Giles, P.—*Manual of Comparative Philology for Classical Students.* 2nd ed. Macmillan, 1901.

This admirable work, which has been translated into German, entirely supersedes all previous summaries of the history of the Greek and Latin languages. It includes also an excellent account of the principles of the science, with an application of these principles to syntax, a field which is only beginning to be worked on the lines of the newer philology. Considerable attention is given to English.

Clark, J.—*Manual of Linguistics.* Thin, 1893.

This book is much slighter than Giles's, but has some very good material, and deals with English more fully in proportion.

3. *Germanic.*

Henry, V.—*Comparative Grammar of English and German.* Sonnenschein, 1894.

Those whose knowledge is mostly confined to modern languages can study the principles of linguistics to excellent purpose within the narrow field of Germanic, as is shown in these lectures above. Prof. Henry, of Paris, is a thoroughly trustworthy writer.

West, A. S.—*Elements of English Grammar.* Cambridge University Press. 8th edition, 1902.
An excellent sketch of historical English.

Toller, T. N.—*Outlines of the History of the English Language.* Cambridge University Press. 1900.
A very sound and readable summary.

Mayhew, A. L.—*Synopsis of Old English Phonology.* Clarendon Press, 1891.

An exceedingly compact account of the relations between English sounds and those corresponding to them in cognate languages.

Behaghel, O.—*Short Historical Grammar of the German Language.* Translated and adapted by Dr E. Trechmann. Macmillan, 1891.

Wright, J.—*Primer of the Gothic Language.* Clarendon Press, 2nd edition, 1899.

The study of these cognate Germanic dialects, the second-cousin and the great-aunt, respectively, of modern English, will of course greatly enlarge the understanding of our own language.

E. LANGUAGE AND PRIMITIVE HISTORY.

1. *General*

Rendall, G. H.—*The Cradle of the Aryans.* Macmillan, 1889.

A sound little *résumé* for its date, but very much has been done in the past fourteen years.

Taylor, I.—*The Origin of the Aryans.* Scott, 1889.

On a larger scale than Rendall's essay, this book is necessarily more out of date, especially on the linguistic side. I am not competent to criticise its craniology and archaeology. Canon Taylor did excellent service by popularising newer views, and the book may still be used with profit if carefully checked by later work.

Schrader, O. (tr. Dr F. B. Jevons).—*Prehistoric Antiquities of the Aryan Peoples.* 1890.

This important work has been superseded by Dr Schrader's recent *Reallexikon*, a dictionary of words bearing on the culture of primeval times. The author is decidedly the leading specialist on linguistic palaeontology.

There is also an excellent account of the controversy in French by S. Reinach: *L'Origine des Aryens* (Leroux, 1892).

2. *Religions.*

Steuding, H.—*Greek and Roman Mythology and Heroic Legend.* (Temple Primers.) Dent, 1901.

An excellent little manual.

Hopkins, E. W.—*The Religions of India.* Arnold, 1896.

De la Saussaye, P. D. C.—*The Religion of the Teutons.* Ginn, 1902.

These two works, in Prof. Jastrow's "Handbooks on the History of Religions," give admirable accounts of religions which, with the Greek, the Roman, and the Persian, supply our main evidence for deducing the religion of the primeval Indogerman.

Ridgeway, W.—*The Early Age of Greece.* Cambridge University Press, 1901 (vol. i.), 1903 (vol. ii.—in the press).

This brilliant work, frequently referred to above, contains very important discussions on the history of Greek and Roman religion, as well as on the origin of their culture. I abstain of course from pronouncing on the archaeologists' debate of which this book is the centre.

Chadwick, H. M.—*The Oak and the Thunder-god.* Harrison, 1900.

A paper presented to the Anthropological Institute, giving an excellent account of the evidence for the cult described on p. 52 above. My lecture was in print before I saw Mr Chadwick's paper, from which I venture to dissent only in the account he gives of the rationale of the link between the oak and the thunder.

3. *Anthropology.*

Tylor, E. B.—*Anthropology.* Macmillan, 1895.

Frazer, J. G.—*The Golden Bough.* 2nd ed., 3 vols., Macmillan, 1901.

Prof. Tylor's manual has chapters on Language, and on the various elements of culture which are taken up from the other side by linguistic palaeontology. Dr Frazer's famous book illustrates phenomena of language very freely, and its study of comparative institutions must be taken into account whenever we examine what the evidence from language proves.

INDEX I.

Names of modern writers are in italics. For convenience, the names of foreign scholars are given with initials only.

Ablaut—*see* Vowel-gradation.
Accent 13 f, 21, 25
Accidental similarities 16, 39
Achaeans 35, 37, 48, 50, 52
Acorns 53
Agriculture 46 f
Albanian 6, 52
Analogy 23 ff
Ancestor-worship 49 ff
Angel, for ancestor spirit 50
Animals, Indogermanic 42
Anthropology 30, 62
Archaeology 30, 35, 45 f, 53
Armenian 6, 42, 45
Articulation and inherited speech-organs 21
Aryan—*see* Indogermanic.
Aryan (=Indo-Iranian) 6 f, 37 f, 40 ff, 45, 47
Asia as Indogerman home 38, 45
Assyrian 39
Athenians 35, 48
Athens, St Paul at 53
Avesta 51

Babylonians 39
Baltic 34 f, 42
Behaghel, O. 60
Blood-offerings 50
Blood revenge 49
Bopp, F. 5

Borrowing of culture words 32
Botany 30, 41
Bradley, H. 57
Bréal, M. 57
Brugmann, Karl 13 f, 58
Burning and burying 50

Cambridgeshire 19
Celt—*see* Keltic.
Chadwick, H. M. 62
Chaucer 25
Clan 49
Clark, J. 59
Classical philology 5, 58 f
Colour words 27
Comparative mythology 11 f
      ,,   syntax 58 f
Conquest, effects on language 23, 36, 38
Conscious phonetic change 10
Conway, Prof. 20, 58
Copper 44 f
Cowell, Prof. ix f
Craniology 30
Curtius, Georg 11 f
Cyrus 36

Dawn-goddess 12
Decimal system 39
Delbrück, B. 58
Dialect mixture 20
Dialects, growth of 22

Dialects of English 19
Diêus Perqûnos 43, 52, 54
Digamma 12
Dirt and religion 52
Dodona 52
Druids 43
"Dug-outs" 43
Duodecimal system 39
Dutch 8

Eastern and Western Indogermans 6, 14, 17, 38
Educational value of Language 2
English Language 8, 18 ff, 25, 27, 56 f, 59 f
Epirus 52
Eschatology 50
Ethnology 30
Etymology 1 f, 9, 34, 56 f
Europe as Indogerman home 38 ff
European races 34 f, 37, 53
Exceptions to phonetic law 15 f

Fakirs 52
"False" Analogy 23
Family life 48 f
Fatherhood, divine 50, 52 f
Fick, A. 36
Finnish 37, 55
Fishing 32, 43 f
Five, word for 14
Formal Analogy 24
Frazer, Dr J. G. 62

Gauls 50
Geology 30
German 8, 10
Germanic languages and peoples 7, 9, 13, 18, 27, 34 f, 38 ff, 43 f, 48, 50, 59 f

Germans, in Linguistics and English studies 4 f, 58
Giles, P. ix, 56 ff
Gipsies, Indogermans as 46
Gold 44
Gothic 4, 32 f, 60
Greek 2 f, 6, 8, 12, 16, 25 f, 32 f, 38, 45, 49
Greek religion 37, 49, 52 ff, 61
Grimm, Jacob 7
Grimm's Law 7 ff, 13, 18 f
Gutturals 14

Hand, name for 33, 45
Hearth 46
Heaven and earth 50 f
Hebrew 16
Henry, V. 59
Herodotus 51
High Germans 10
Hirt, H. 41
Home life 46
Homer 35, 48, 52
Homicide 49
Hopkins, E. W. 61
Horace 20
Horse 14, 34
House-master and -mistress 46

India, northern immigrants into 36, 49
Indian languages 6, 34
Indogermanic, the name 7
,,   peoples, their home 34 ff
,,   , eastern and western 6, 14, 17, 38
,,   , sounds of 9, 13
,,   , cautions in reconstructing 14 f

Indogermanic religion 49 ff
Invariability of phonetic law 15 ff
Ionians 35
Iranian 6, 34, 36
Isles of the Blest 50
Italic 6, 20, 34, 43, 45

Jastrow, M. 61
Jevons, Dr F. B. 61
Jones, Sir W. 3 ff

Kellett, E. E. ix
Keltic 4, 6, 18, 34 f, 38, 43, 45
Kluge F. 57

Lake-dwellers 43 f
Language, as a Science 1
,, its educational value 2
,, and Race 38
Latham, Dr R. G. 38 f
Latin 3 f, 6, 8, 16, 19, 27, 32, 38
Law in Language 12, 15
Letts 44
Leskien, A. 15
Lightning 52
Linguistic Palaeontology 30 ff
Lithuanian 6 f, 34, 42, 52
"Little Year" 48
Logical Analogy 24
"Long hundred" 39
Loss of old words 32, 43 ff
Lutz, F. 57
Lunar year 47
Lystra, St Paul at 53

MacAdam 26
Manes (Lat.) 49
Marriage 49
Material Analogy 24
Matriarchate 48
Mayhew, A. L. 59

Media 37
Mediterranean race 35, 38, 48 ff
Metals 44 f
Milton 28
Müller, Prof. Max 9, 11
Murray, Dr J. A. H. 57

Nature-worship 50
Neogrammarians viii, 15, 58
Neolithic culture 45
Nomadic life 46
Norse 8, 52
North European Race 35, 37 f, 48 ff
Numerals 33, 39

Oak-tree and thunder 41, 52, 62
Oertel, H. 56
One, word for 33
Ossetes 36

Pastoral life 46
Patricians at Rome 36, 49
Paul, H. 55
Paul, St 53
Peile, Dr J. v, viii f
Pelasgians 35, 38
Persians 36, 50 ff, 61
Phonetic change, unconscious 10 f
Plough 47
Poseidon 37, 52
Postgate, Dr J. P. 57
Primitive Indogerman home 34, 38 ff
,, ,, religion 37, 49 ff, 61 f
,, ,, animals 42
,, ,, metals 44 f
Psychology in Language 2, 28
Purchase of wife 49

Race and Language 38

Races of Europe 34 f, 37, 53
Rapidity of utterance 20 f
Reinach, S. 61
Relationship words 48
Religion of Indogermans 49 ff
Rendall, Dr G. H. 60
Ridgeway, Prof. vii, 35 ff, 39, 43, 48 f, 52, 61
Roman ancestor-worship 49
Romance languages 6
Rouse, Dr W. H. D. 58

Sabine 20, 36
Sanskrit 3, 6, 17, 40, 44
Saussaye, P. D. C. de la 61
Schleicher, August 13 ff
Schmidt, Johannes 39, 45
Schrader, O. 53, 61
Sea 41
Semantics 33, 41, 57 f
Semites 45
Sexagesimal system 39
Silver 45
Simplification of language 28
Sixty 39
Skeat, Prof. 19, 56
Sky and Oak 52, 62
Slavonic 6, 34, 42, 44
Sonant liquids and nasals 13, 21
Sound-shifting 10, 18
Speech-mixture 23
Spirits 49, 51, 53
"Sporadic" change 12
Spring 40, 47
Steppes, migration over 44, 47
Steuding, H. 61
Stone Age 44
Strong, Logeman and Wheeler 55
Strong perfect, English and Greek 25
Sweet, Dr H. 37, 55

Syntax 58 f

Tacitus 48
Taylor, Dr I. 57, 60
Thera 50
Thunder-god 41, 52, 62
Toller, Prof. 59
Trechmann, Dr 60
Trees, argument from 40 f
Tree-names 27, 33, 40 f
Twelfth Night 48
Tylor, Prof. 62

Ulfilas—*see* Wulfila.
Umbrian 33

Vedic Sanskrit 6, 13, 51 f
Verner's Law 13
Vocabulary of primitive speech 31 ff
Vowel-gradation 24 f
Vowels, Indogermanic 13

Wergild 49
Wesley 28
West, A. S. 59
Whitney, W. D. 56
Winter 40
Women, condition of 48
Wright, Prof. 58, 60
Writing 58
Wulfila 33

Year, length of 47

Zend 40
Zeus 37, 50 ff
„ of the Oak 43, 54
Zoology 30
Zoroaster 51
Zulus 21

INDEX II.

In this word-index the words in italics are those quoted as representing Indogermanic originals.

accent 21
Achilles (Gr.) 36
Agilulfs (old Ger.) 36
ai (Fr.) 25
aime (Fr.) 25
alnus (Lat.) 27
amo (Lat.) 25
Aurora (Lat.) 3
avons (Fr.) 25

bear 26
beech 33
"beek" 25, 28
began, begun 28
beseeched 24
bhrātar (Skt.) 8
birch 41
blue 27
book 25
bore 26
bough 18
brother 8, 48
Bruder (Ger.) 8
brung 26

call 8
cook 46
corn 46
cover 16
cow 46

daughter 32, 34, 48
deism 16
despot 46
deus (Lat.) 16, 51
Digentia (Lat.) 20
divinus (Lat.) 51
dog 32
domus (Lat.) 46
dough 18
drownded 28
Dyaus (Skt.) 50 f

ear 47
Easter 3
either 27
eleven 39
equos (Lat.) 34
Erin (Ir.) 7
-ētum (Lat.) 27
ewe 46

father 18, 32 ff, 48
feet 25, 28
female 27
fir 41
fish 32, 43
five 14, 27
flavos (Lat.) 27
flay 39
foot 25, 33

four 27
frater (Lat.) 8
fraxinus (Lat.) 41

Gast (Ger.) 17
Gerste (Ger.) 46
guest 17

health 27
helvos (Lat.) 27
hiemps (Lat.) 40
Himâ(laya) (Skt.) 40
hither 27
hōrā (Gr.) 47
hound 32
hundred 33

iasc (Ir.) 43
ice 40
ingens (Lat.) 3
iron 44
-ise 26
isi (Zend) 40
ἴσμεν (Gr.) 25
-ize, see -ise

Jove (Lat.) 50

καλῶ (Gr.) 9
kâphar (Heb.) 16
knave 3

larch 19
larix (Lat.) 19
lenger (M. E.) 25
Licenza (Ital.) 20
lingua 19 f
loaf 47
loch 14
long 25
Lough 18

macadamise 26
male 27
mare (Lat.) 41
mead 42
Medise 26
mere 41 f
mill 47
month 47
mother 32 f, 48

neither 27
nescius (Lat.) 3
nice 3
nicht (Ger.) 14
north, northern 27

odor (Lat.) 19
οἶδα, οἴδαμεν (Gr.) 25
olêre (Lat.) 19 f
onto(logy) 3
oven 46

parabolo (Lat.) 25
paraçus (Skt.) 39
parole, parlons (Fr.) 25
*parri*cide 49
pater 49
πέλεκυς (Gr.) 39
perhaps, p'raps 20
Perqûnos (Indog.) 52
Pfund (Ger.) 19
φράτηρ (Gr.) 8
pilaqqu (Assyr.) 39
pînus (Lat.) 27
piscis (Lat.) 43
plecto (Lat.) 39
plough 18
pondus (Lat.) 19
praedico (Lat.) 19
preach 19, 24
predige (Ger.) 19

(pre)sent 3

quercus (Lat.) 41
quern 47

raught 24, 28
reach 24
red 44
right 20
righteous 20
right-you-are 20

sang 25, 27 f
sat 25, 27
scrope 26
sew 47
silly 3
sister 32 48
sit 25, 27
snow 40
-snus (Lat.) 27
son 32, 48
sooth 3
sore 24
sorrow 24
sorry 24
sounded 28
south, southern 27
sow 47
steer 46
Strasse (Ger.) 19
strâta (Lat.) 18
street 19
sung 25, 27 f
suppose, s'pose 20
suttee (Skt.) 3

tar 41

taught 28
teached 24
tear 26
theism 16
θεός (Gr.) 16, 51, 53
thither 27
timber 46
tongue 19
tore 26
tree 20, 33, 41
Tues(day) 50 f
twelve 39
two 33

uncouth 3

venons (Fr.) 25
ver (Lat.) 40
viens (Fr.) 25

wagon 46
warm 17
weal, wealth 27
wear 26
weave 47
wed 49
widow 49
wit, witen 25
wore 26
-wos (Lat. and Prim. Ger.) 27
wot 25
writ, wrote 25

year 47
yellow 27, 44

Zeus (Gr.) 50 f
Zimmer (Ger.) 46

For EU product safety concerns, contact us at Calle de José Abascal, 56–1°,
28003 Madrid, Spain or eugpsr@cambridge.org.

www.ingramcontent.com/pod-product-compliance
Ingram Content Group UK Ltd.
Pitfield, Milton Keynes, MK11 3LW, UK
UKHW012334130625
459647UK00009B/273